WITHDRAWAL

INSIDE THE NBA

HOUSTON ROCKETS

Sam Moussavi and Samantha Nugent

AV2 BY WEIGL
MEDIA ENHANCED BOOKS
ADDED VALUE · AUDIO VISUAL

AV² provides enriched content that supplements and complements this book. Weigl's AV² books strive to create inspired learning and engage young minds in a total learning experience.

Your AV² Media Enhanced books come alive with...

Audio
Listen to sections of the book read aloud.

Key Words
Study vocabulary, and complete a matching word activity.

Video
Watch informative video clips.

Quizzes
Test your knowledge.

Embedded Weblinks
Gain additional information for research.

Slide Show
View images and captions, and prepare a presentation.

Try This!
Complete activities and hands-on experiments.

... and much, much more!

Go to **www.av2books.com**, and enter this book's unique code.

BOOK CODE

J333986

AV² **by Weigl** brings you media enhanced books that support active learning.

Published by AV² by Weigl
350 5th Avenue, 59th Floor
New York, NY 10118
Website: www.av2books.com

Library of Congress Control Number: 2016935101

ISBN 978-1-4896-4691-0 (hardcover)
ISBN 978-1-4896-5062-7 (softcover)
ISBN 978-1-4896-4692-7 (multi-user eBook)

Printed in the United States of America in Brainerd, Minnesota
1 2 3 4 5 6 7 8 9 0 20 19 18 17 16

052016
200516

Project Coordinator Heather Kissock
Art Director Terry Paulhus

Photo Credits
Every reasonable effort has been made to trace ownership and to obtain permission to reprint copyright material. The publishers would be pleased to have any errors or omissions brought to their attention so that they may be corrected in subsequent printings.

Weigl acknowledges Getty Images and iStock as its primary image suppliers for this title.

HOUSTON ROCKETS

CONTENTS

AV² Book Code. 2
Introduction 4
History 6
The Arena. 8
Where They Play 10
The Uniforms 12
The Coaches 14
The Mascot 16
Superstars. 18
The Greatest of All Time 20
The Moment 22
All-Time Records 24
Timeline 26
Write a Biography 28
Trivia Time 30
Key Words/Index 31
www.av2books.com. 32

Introduction

In the mid-1990s, the Houston Rockets brought two NBA Championships to southeastern Texas. As a result, the team earned the nickname "Clutch City." This meant that when it counted most, the Rockets were able to pull through to the win. The **franchise** has enjoyed success, making it to the Western **Conference Playoffs** in 28 **seasons** since moving to Houston in 1971.

There have been struggles along the way. From trying to replace coach Rudy Tomjanovich, to recovering from the loss of a key player, the Rockets franchise has seen its share of ups and downs. So far, Houston has been able to consistently rebuild.

Josh Smith is a new addition to the Rockets. He joined the team in 2015, after previously playing with the Hawks, the Pistons, and the Clippers.

Today, the Rockets franchise is led by another superstar, James Harden. Harden looks to lead the Rockets back to the NBA Finals, like the Rockets' superstars before him. Complete with a strong cast of teammates, Houston made it to the Western Conference Finals in 2015. This may be the year the team brings another NBA title to "Clutch City."

Shooting guard James Harden won a gold medal as a member of the 2012 U.S. Men's Olympic basketball team.

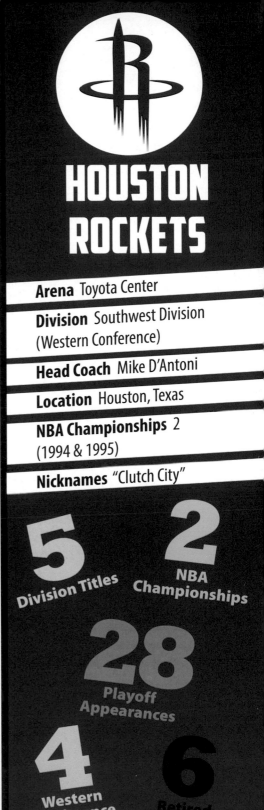

HOUSTON ROCKETS

Arena Toyota Center

Division Southwest Division (Western Conference)

Head Coach Mike D'Antoni

Location Houston, Texas

NBA Championships 2 (1994 & 1995)

Nicknames "Clutch City"

5 Division Titles

2 NBA Championships

28 Playoff Appearances

4 Western Conference Championships

6 Retired Numbers

History

The Rockets have had **16 All-Star players** in their history.

During the 1980–81 season, the Rockets were ranked 11th out of 23 teams. Moses Malone led the entire league in rebounds per game, with nearly 15.

The Rockets franchise was founded in 1967 in San Diego, California. The San Diego Rockets joined the National Basketball Association (NBA) as an **expansion franchise** before the 1967–68 season. The team played in San Diego until moving to Houston before the 1971–72 season.

Led by guard Calvin Murphy in the mid-1970s, the Rockets made it to the Western Conference Finals for the first time in their history in 1977. Center Moses Malone helped lead the Rockets to their first NBA Finals in 1981. The team lost in six games to the Boston Celtics. After another NBA Finals loss in 1986, the Rockets had a string of eight seasons where they did not make it past the first round of the playoffs.

In 1994, led by coach Rudy Tomjanovich and center Hakeem Olajuwon, the Rockets won their first of two back-to-back NBA Championships. After Olajuwon left the Rockets in 2001, the team experienced a period of rebuilding before getting young players Tracy McGrady and Yao Ming, both of whom brought tough defense and unparalleled height. Now the Rockets are led by Harden, and center Dwight Howard. The team is looking to bring Houston its first NBA title since 1995.

When Houston won the NBA Finals in 1994, it was only the second Finals series to go to game 7.

The Arena

The Toyota Center is the **26th largest** arena in the NBA.

Toyota paid $100 million dollars to have its name on the arena.

The San Diego Rockets played their home games at the 14,400-seat San Diego Sports Arena from 1967 to 1971. When the Rockets moved to Houston at the beginning of the 1971–72 season, they did not have their own **home arena**. During that first season in Houston, the Rockets played their home games at several arenas including the Astrodome, AstroHall, and Sam Houston Coliseum. During their second season in Houston, the team took the Hofheinz Pavilion on the University of Houston campus as their home. The Rockets played there for three more seasons.

The Rockets moved to the Summit in downtown Houston in 1975, and stayed there for the next 28 seasons. The Summit was the Rockets' home during their two championship seasons in the mid-1990s. In 2010, The Summit was purchased by a church group and is now a house of worship.

The team moved into the Toyota Center before the 2003–04 season, and it still plays all of its home games there. The arena is located in downtown Houston and seats 18,055 fans. At the Toyota Center during the 2007–08 season, the Rockets achieved a franchise best 22-game winning streak.

The Toyota Center spans six city blocks in downtown Houston.

Where They Play

British Columbia

Alberta

Saskatchewan

Manitoba

Ontario

CAN

Washington

Montana

North Dakota

Minnesota

7

Wisconsin

25

9

Oregon

Idaho

South Dakota

Iowa

21

5

Nevada

Wyoming

Nebraska

Illinois

10

UNITED

Utah

Colorado

6

Kansas

Missouri

1

California

STATES

2

8

Oklahoma

13

Arkansas

3

Arizona

New Mexico

4

Pacific Ocean

MEXICO

11

Texas

Mi

15

12

Louisiana

Toyota Center, Houston

Gulf of Mexico

NBA WESTERN CONFERENCE

PACIFIC DIVISION
1. Golden State Warriors
2. Los Angeles Clippers
3. Los Angeles Lakers
4. Phoenix Suns
5. Sacramento Kings

NORTHWEST DIVISION
6. Denver Nuggets
7. Minnesota Timberwolves
8. Oklahoma City Thunder
9. Portland Trail Blazers
10. Utah Jazz

SOUTHWEST DIVISION
11. Dallas Mavericks
★ 12. Houston Rockets
13. Memphis Grizzlies
14. New Orleans Pelicans
15. San Antonio Spurs

TOYOTA CENTER

Arena
Toyota Center

Location
1510 Polk Street
Houston, Texas 77002

Broke Ground
2001

Completed
2003

Features
- Seats 18,055
- First regular season game took place on October 30, 2003
- Cost $235 million to build

LEGEND
☆ Toyota Center
■ Western Conference
■ Eastern Conference

Newfoundland
Quebec
Prince Edward Island
New Brunswick
New Hampshire
Vermont
Maine
Nova Scotia
Massachusetts
Rhode Island
Connecticut
New York
New Jersey
Michigan
Pennsylvania
Ohio
Delaware
Maryland
Indiana
West Virginia
Virginia
District of Columbia
Kentucky
North Carolina
Tennessee
South Carolina
Alabama
Georgia
Florida

Atlantic Ocean

N
W E
S

SOUTHEAST DIVISION
16. Atlanta Hawks
17. Charlotte Hornets
18. Miami Heat
19. Orlando Magic
20. Washington Wizards

CENTRAL DIVISION
21. Chicago Bulls
22. Cleveland Cavaliers
23. Detroit Pistons
24. Indiana Pacers
25. Milwaukee Bucks

ATLANTIC DIVISION
26. Boston Celtics
27. Brooklyn Nets
28. New York Knicks
29. Philadelphia 76ers
30. Toronto Raptors

NBA EASTERN CONFERENCE

The Uniforms

The Rockets played **three games** during the 2014–15 season in their **alternate Chinese-inspired uniforms** to celebrate the Lunar New Year.

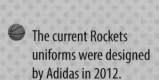 The current Rockets uniforms were designed by Adidas in 2012.

HOME

While the franchise played in San Diego, its primary colors were green and gold. The home uniform was white with "Rockets" across the chest. The away uniform was green with "San Diego" across the chest.

A new color combination of red and yellow came with the move to Houston. The team wore the same uniforms from 1972 to 1996 with only minor adjustments. Both the white home and red away uniforms had yellow trim, with "Houston" across the front. In 1996, the Rockets drastically changed their logo and uniforms, making navy blue the primary color.

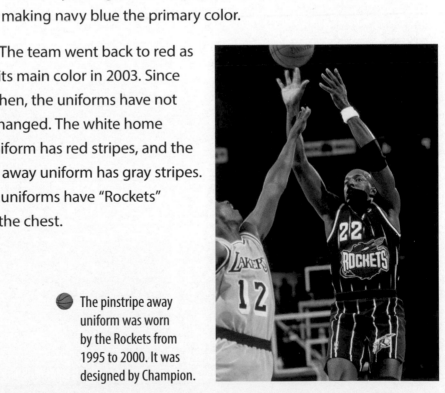

AWAY

The team went back to red as its main color in 2003. Since then, the uniforms have not changed. The white home uniform has red stripes, and the red away uniform has gray stripes. Both uniforms have "Rockets" across the chest.

🏀 The pinstripe away uniform was worn by the Rockets from 1995 to 2000. It was designed by Champion.

The Coaches

The Rockets won **55** games during **Rudy Tomjanovich's** first full season as coach in 1992–93.

Before coming to the Rockets, Bickerstaff was an assistant coach with the Charlotte Bobcats and Minnesota Timberwolves.

The Houston Rockets franchise has had 13 head coaches in its 49-year existence. The team has been coached by some of the most well-known names in NBA history. Successful coaches Tex Winter, Del Harris, Bill Fitch, and Jeff Van Gundy have all coached the Rockets. Former NBA players Don Chaney, Rick Adelman, and Kevin McHale have coached the team as well.

BILL FITCH Bill Fitch became the head coach of the Houston Rockets in 1983, after leading the Boston Celtics to an NBA title in 1981. In 1986, he led the Rockets, with centers Olajuwon and Ralph Sampson, to the NBA Finals. Fitch coached the Rockets for five seasons and finished with 216 wins.

RUDY TOMJANOVICH Rudy Tomjanovich played 11 years in the NBA, all with the Rockets franchise. He became the head coach of the Rockets in 1992. In 1994, he led the team to its first NBA Championship. In 1995, he won a second straight NBA title with the team. Tomjanovich won a franchise record 503 games in 12 seasons as Rockets coach.

J. B. BICKERSTAFF J.B. Bickerstaff replaced Kevin McHale as the head coach of the Rockets at the beginning of the 2015–16 season. He was named the team's **interim coach** for the rest of the season. Bickerstaff was an **assistant coach** in the NBA for 12 seasons before taking over the Rockets.

The Mascot

Clutch has his very own rock song, "Clutch the Bear," available for purchase wherever music is sold.

Based on the team's nickname, Clutch the Rocket Bear was introduced on March 14, 1995. Clutch is easy to spot. He is the large teddy bear wearing Rockets gear during games at the Toyota Center. He has a big belly and a friendly face.

Clutch performs many different acts during halftimes and timeouts, and he is also known for his activities outside the stadium. He appears at charity events around the city of Houston. Clutch hosts his annual Children's Charity Christmas Party every December. The party gives Clutch and Rockets players the chance to spend time with kids from the city of Houston.

fun facts

#1 Clutch was named the fifth most recognizable mascot in sports by *USA Today* in February 2005.

#2 In 2006, Clutch the Rocket Bear was inducted into the Mascot Hall of Fame in Whiting, Indiana.

Superstars

Many talented players have suited up for the Rockets. A few of them have become icons of the team and the city it represents.

Moses Malone

Moses Malone joined the Houston Rockets through a trade with the Buffalo Braves early in the 1976–77 season. Known mostly as a **rebounder** and defender, Malone also showed his offensive skills during the 1978–79 season. He averaged 24.8 **points**, 1.5 **block**s, and 17.6 rebounds per game that season, winning the NBA's MVP award. Malone led the Rockets to the NBA Finals in 1981, where they lost in six games to the Boston Celtics. He played six seasons in Houston and made five playoff appearances for the team. Malone passed away in 2015.

Position: Center
NBA Seasons: 19 (1976–1995)
Born: March 23, 1955, Petersburg, Virginia

Elvin Hayes

Position: Center/Power Forward
NBA Seasons: 16 (1968–1984)
Born: November 17, 1945, Rayville, Louisiana

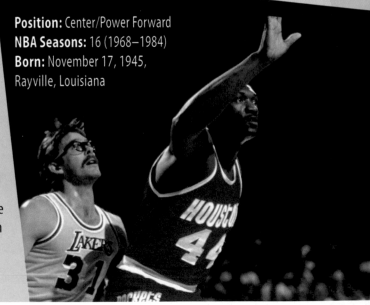

Elvin Hayes exploded onto the NBA scene as a **rookie** with the San Diego Rockets in 1968. In just his 13th game as a pro, Hayes scored a career high 54 points in a win against the Detroit Pistons. He led the NBA in scoring in the 1968–69 season, with 28.4 points per game, along with 17.1 rebounds per game. He was also named to the NBA All-Rookie Team. Hayes played a total of seven seasons with the San Diego and Houston Rockets.

Clyde Drexler

Clyde "The Glyde" Drexler began his career with the Portland Trailblazers before joining the Rockets in a trade during the 1994–95 season. In Houston, he would be reunited with his old college teammate Hakeem Olajuwon, from the University of Houston. Drexler helped the Rockets win a second straight NBA title in 1995, sweeping the Orlando Magic in the NBA Finals. He played four total seasons in Houston, averaging 19 points, 6 rebounds, and 5 assists per game before retiring from the NBA.

Position: Shooting Guard/Small Forward
NBA Seasons: 15 (1983–1998)
Born: June 22, 1962, New Orleans, Louisiana

James Harden

James Harden was traded to the Houston Rockets from the Oklahoma City Thunder before the start of the 2012–13 season. Harden was a key member off the Thunder bench, helping the team reach the 2012 NBA Finals. He became a star in Houston right away, leading the Rockets in points, and guiding them to the NBA Playoffs for the first time since 2009. Nicknamed "The Beard" for his outrageous facial hair, Harden led the Rockets to the Western Conference Finals in 2015.

Position: Shooting Guard
NBA Seasons: 7 (2009–present)
Born: August 26, 1989, Los Angeles, California

The Moment

In the 1994 playoffs, Olajuwon scored a total of 664 points.

The greatest moment in Houston Rockets history came during the second half of game 3 of the Western Conference Semifinals in the 1994 Playoffs. The Rockets went against the Phoenix Suns and league MVP Charles Barkley. Houston lost the first two games of the series at home, and was in danger of going down three games to none in Phoenix.

The Rockets were down eight points at the half. When the game started to turn in the third quarter, sharpshooter Vernon Maxwell scored 31 points in the second half, and Olajuwon scored 26 for the game. The team also received contributions from Robert Horry, Sam Cassell, Mario Elie, and Kenny Smith on the way to a 77-point second half.

The Rockets won game 3 in Phoenix by 16 points. Maxwell finished with 34 points, and Olajuwon had 26 points and 15 rebounds. The Rockets went on to win the series against Phoenix in seven games. Success in the series gave Houston the confidence to win its NBA Championship a month later.

The Rockets won their first NBA Championship against the New York Knicks in 1994.

After the NBA Championship win, fans rushed the court and celebrated peacefully in the streets of the city.

All-Time Records

26,511

Most Points in Franchise History
Hakeem Olajuwon racked up 26,511 points over the course of his 17-year career with the Rockets.

503

13,382

Most Total Rebounds in Franchise History
Hakeem Olajuwon had 13,382 total rebounds during his Rockets career. He owns many Rockets franchise records.

57

Most Regular Season Coaching Wins

Rudy Tomjanovich won a franchise record 503 games over 12 seasons as the Rockets' coach.

12 Highest Field Goal Percentage During a Single Season

Otis Thorpe hit 59 percent of his shots during the 1991–92 season, a single season record.

Most Points Scored in a Game

Calvin Murphy scored a franchise-record 57 points against the New Jersey Nets on March 18, 1978.

26.5 Highest Points Per Game Average

James Harden has averaged 26.5 points per game during his four years with the Rockets, the highest points per game average in Rockets history.

Timeline

Throughout the team's history, the Rockets have had many memorable events that have become defining moments for the team and its fans.

1971

The team moves to Houston, Texas, before the 1971–72 season, and from then on are known as the Houston Rockets.

1967

The San Diego Rockets join the NBA as an expansion franchise before the 1967–68 season.

1969

The San Diego Rockets reach the NBA Playoffs for the first time in franchise history.

1960   **1970**   **1980**

1975

The Rockets make the NBA Playoffs for the first time since moving to Houston from San Diego. The team makes it to the second round of the playoffs before losing to Boston.

1976–1977

With newcomer Malone and veterans Murphy and Tomjanovich, the Rockets win their first division title ever and make it to the Conference Finals before losing to the Philadelphia 76ers.

1981

Led by Murphy, Malone, and coach Del Harris, the Rockets make their first ever NBA Finals appearance in 1981. They lose to Larry Bird and the Boston Celtics in six games.

The Future

Looking to build from previous Conference Finals appearances, the Rockets have made some recent coaching changes. The team has plenty of talent in Harden, Howard, Trevor Ariza, and Patrick Beverly to get back on track in the Western Conference.

2015

The Rockets make it to the 2015 Western Conference Finals for the first time since 1997.

1994

The Rockets win their first NBA Championship in franchise history, beating the New York Knicks in seven games. Olajuwon is named NBA Finals MVP, outplaying Knicks star center Patrick Ewing.

1990   **2000**   **2010**   **2020**

2002

The Houston Rockets select center Yao Ming with the first overall pick in the 2002 NBA Draft. Ming is the first Chinese player ever selected number one overall. He plays eight seasons with the Rockets, making eight All-Star teams.

1995

The Rockets win a second NBA Championship in a row, this time defeating the Orlando Magic in a four-game sweep. Olajuwon is once again named Finals MVP.

Write a Biography

Life Story

A person's life story can be the subject of a book. This kind of book is called a biography. Biographies often describe the lives of people who have achieved great success. These people may be alive today, or they may have lived many years ago. Reading a biography can help you learn more about a great person.

Get the Facts

Use this book, and research in the library and on the internet, to find out more about your favorite star. Learn as much about this player as you can. What position does he play? What are his statistics in important categories? Has he set any records? Also, be sure to write down key events in the person's life. What was his childhood like? What has he accomplished off the court? Is there anything else that makes this person special or unusual?

Use the Concept Web

A concept web is a useful research tool. Read the questions in the concept web on the following page. Answer the questions in your notebook. Your answers will help you write a biography.

Concept Web

Adulthood
- Where does this individual currently reside?
- Does he or she have a family?

Your Opinion
- What did you learn from the books you read in your research?
- Would you suggest these books to others?
- Was anything missing from these books?

Childhood
- Where and when was this person born?
- Describe his or her parents, siblings, and friends.
- Did this person grow up in unusual circumstances?

Accomplishments off the Court
- What is this person's life's work?
- Has he or she received awards or recognition for accomplishments?
- How have this person's accomplishments served others?

Write a Biography

Help and Obstacles
- Did this individual have a positive attitude?
- Did he or she receive help from others?
- Did this person have a mentor?
- Did this person face any hardships?
- If so, how were the hardships overcome?

Accomplishments on the Court
- What records does this person hold?
- What key games and plays have defined his career?
- What are his stats in categories important to his position?

Work and Preparation
- What was this person's education?
- What was his or her work experience?
- How does this person work?
- What is the process he or she uses?

Trivia Time

Take this quiz to test your knowledge of the Houston Rockets.
The answers are printed upside down under each question.

1 Where did the Rockets franchise begin?

A. San Diego, California

2 What year did the Rockets win their first NBA Championship?

A. 1994

3 Which coach led the Rockets to two NBA Championships?

A. Rudy Tomjanovich

4 What is the Houston Rockets' nickname?

A. "Clutch City"

5 How many seasons did Clyde Drexler play for the Houston Rockets?

A. 4

6 Which coach led the Rockets to their first NBA Finals appearance in 1981?

A. Del Harris

7 What year did "Clutch" the Rocket Bear become the Rockets' mascot?

A. 1995

8 How many games did Bill Fitch win as coach of the Houston Rockets?

A. 216

9 How many times has Hakeem Olajuwon won the NBA Finals MVP award?

A. Two, 1994 and 1995

10 How many points per game has James Harden averaged over the course of his four years with the team?

A. 26.5 points per game

11 What is Hakeem Olajuwon's nickname?

A. "The Dream"

12 What was the name of the coach who took over for Kevin McHale at the start of the 2015–16 season?

A. J.B. Bickerstaff

Key Words

assistant coach: a coach who helps the head coach with running practice, drawing up plays, and devising strategies

blocks: when a defensive player taps an offensive player's shot out of the air and stops it from getting to the basket

conference: an association of sports teams that play each other

expansion franchise: a team that joins a sports league after play has begun. An expansion franchise is not a part of the original group of teams in a new league.

franchise: a team that is a member of a professional sports league

home arena: the venue where a basketball team plays its home games

interim coach: a coach that fills in for the head coach when he leaves the position

playoffs: a series of games that occur after regular season play

points: any basket that is scored from the free throw line, inside of the three point line, or outside the three point line

rebounder: a player who retrieves the ball after either a player on his own team or player on the other team misses a shot

rookie: a member of a team in his or her first full season in that sport

seasons: games played that count on a team's win-loss record. In the NBA, teams play 82 games during the season.

Index

Adelman, Rick 15
Ariza, Trevor 27

Beverly, Patrick 27
Bickerstaff, J. B. 5, 14, 15, 30

Cassell, Sam 23
Clutch the Rocket Bear 16, 17, 30

Drexler, Clyde 19, 30

Elie, Mario 23

Fitch, Bill 15, 30

Harden, James 5, 7, 19, 25, 27, 30
Hayes, Elvin 18

Malone, Moses 6, 7, 18, 26
Ming, Yao 7, 27
Murphy, Calvin 7, 25, 26

National Basketball Association (NBA) 4, 5, 7, 8, 15, 18, 19, 20, 21, 23, 26, 27, 30

Olajuwon, Hakeem 7, 15, 19, 20, 21, 22, 23, 24, 27, 30

Phoenix Suns 10, 23

San Diego Rockets 7, 9, 18, 26
Southwest Division 5, 10

Thorpe, Otis 25
Tomjanovich, Rudy 4, 7, 14, 15, 25, 26, 30
Toyota Center 5, 8, 9, 10, 11, 17

uniforms 12, 13

Western Conference 4, 5, 7, 11, 19, 20, 23, 27

Log on to www.av2books.com

AV² by Weigl brings you media enhanced books that support active learning. Go to www.av2books.com, and enter the special code found on page 2 of this book. You will gain access to enriched and enhanced content that supplements and complements this book. Content includes video, audio, weblinks, quizzes, a slide show, and activities.

AV² Online Navigation

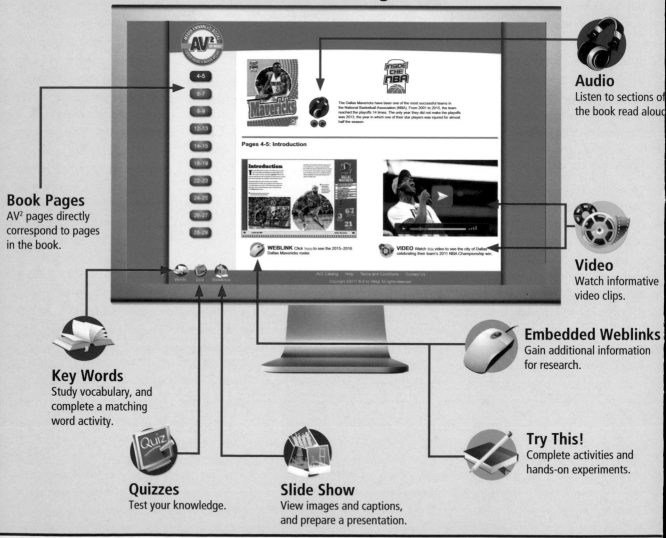

Book Pages
AV² pages directly correspond to pages in the book.

Audio
Listen to sections of the book read aloud.

Video
Watch informative video clips.

Embedded Weblinks
Gain additional information for research.

Key Words
Study vocabulary, and complete a matching word activity.

Try This!
Complete activities and hands-on experiments.

Quizzes
Test your knowledge.

Slide Show
View images and captions, and prepare a presentation.

AV² was built to bridge the gap between print and digital. We encourage you to tell us what you like and what you want to see in the future.

Sign up to be an AV² Ambassador at www.av2books.com/ambassador.

Due to the dynamic nature of the Internet, some of the URLs and activities provided as part of AV² by Weigl may have changed or ceased to exist. AV² by Weigl accepts no responsibility for any such changes. All media enhanced books are regularly monitored to update addresses and sites in a timely manner. Contact AV² by Weigl at 1-866-649-3445 or av2books@weigl.com with any questions, comments, or feedback.

WITHDRAWAL